NO RUINED STONE

SHARA McCALLUM

NO RUINED STONE

Alice James Books
FARMINGTON, MAINE
alicejamesbooks.org

10 9 8 7 6 5 4 3 2 1

Alice James Books are published by Alice James Poetry Cooperative, Inc.,
an affiliate of the University of Maine at Farmington.

Alice James Books
114 Prescott Street
Farmington, ME 04938
www.alicejamesbooks.org

Library of Congress Cataloging-in-Publication Data

Names: McCallum, Shara, 1972- author.
Title: No ruined stone / Shara McCallum.
Description: Farmington, ME : Alice James Books, [2021]
Identifiers: LCCN 2020045538 (print) | LCCN 2020045539 (ebook) | ISBN
    9781948579193 (trade paperback) | ISBN 9781948579438 (epub)
Subjects: LCSH: Burns, Robert, 1759-1796--Poetry. |
    Slavery--Jamaica--Poetry. | LCGFT: Poetry.
Classification: LCC PS3563.C33446 N63 2021 (print) | LCC PS3563.C33446
    (ebook) | DDC 811/.54--dc23
LC record available at https://lccn.loc.gov/2020045538
LC ebook record available at https://lccn.loc.gov/2020045539

Alice James Books gratefully acknowledges support from individual donors, private
foundations, the University of Maine at Farmington, the National Endowment for
the Arts, the Amazon Literary Partnership, and the Maine Arts Commission, an
independent state agency supported by the National Endowment for the Arts.

Cover art: © Calum Colvin

CONTENTS

ISABELLA

For my foremothers and for my daughters

There are plenty of ruined buildings in the world but no ruined stones.

—HUGH MacDIARMID

NO RUINED STONE

May 2018: to Robert Burns, after Calum Colvin's "Portrait of Hugh MacDiarmid"

You saturate the sight
of those who come after, poets
and painters alike. Your words invade
my mind's listening, manacle
my tongue when I try to speak
on all I backward cast my eye
and fear and canna see.
Who would I have been
to you, what stone
in the ruined house of the past?
In this world, I am unloosed, belonging
to no country, no tribe, no clan.
Not African. Not Scotland.
And you, voice that stalks
my waking and dreaming,
you more myth than man,
cannot unmake history.
So why am I here
resurrecting you to speak
when your silence gulfs centuries?
Why do I find myself
on your doorstep, knocking,
when I know the dead
will never answer?

PRIMER

Ayr Mount, Ayrshire, Atlantic, Akan,
Backra, Bannockburn, Burns, Bairns,
Caledonia, Cuffee, Coromantee, Culloden,
Douglas, Duppy, Debtor, Dream,
Empire, Exile, Economics, Emancipation,
Freemason, Fortune, Feared, Freed,
Greenock, Gambit, Glasgow, Greed,
Hadrian, Hero, Highlands, Home,
Island, Inalienable, Insurrection, Independence,
Jamaica, Justice, Jacobite, Joseph
Knight, Kilmarnock, Kingston, Kin,
Lowlands, Leeward, Liberty, Lies,
Merchant, Maroon, Macaulay, Miscegenation,
Nancy, Nanny, Noble, Nation,
Obeah, Overseer, Ossian, Ocean,
Passage, Passing, Profit, Prophet,
Quadroon, Quota, Quashi, Quandary,
Rebellion, Race, Rising, Rape,
Slavery, Springbank, Scotland, Silence,
Tacky, Treaties, Truth, Treason,
Unstoried, Unsung, Unjust, Union,
Voyage, Violence, Victors, Victims,
Windward, Wallace, Wedderburn, West Indian,
Xaymaca, Xenolithic, Xenogenesis, X,
Yonder, Yearning, Yoked, Yield,
Zeitgeist, Zealot, Zero-sum game.

1759

1786

1806

1825

1833

DRAMATIS PERSONAE

Robert Burns Scottish Poet, Bookkeeper at Springbank, Ayr Mount

Gilbert Burns Scotsman, Brother of Robert Burns

Nancy African woman, enslaved at Springbank, Ayr Mount

Charles Douglas Scotsman, "Master" at Springbank, Ayr Mount

Agnes Jamaican "Mulatta"
Daughter of Nancy and Robert Burns

Isabella Jamaican-Scottish "Quadroon"
Daughter of Agnes and Charles Douglas
Granddaughter of Nancy and Robert Burns

Husband Scotsman, Isabella's husband

THE BARD

JAMAICA, 1786-1796

My life reminded me of a ruined temple.

—ROBERT BURNS

AE FOND KISS

What was it I knew then
have now forgotten entirely
was it the parting by the river
that first girl I held at Harvest
or planting season when love
sprung vernal or was it squandered
by the dock at Greenock
where I lay my Mary down or
at sea the last farewell to Jean
when I cast myself out
like a line of fishing wire
pitching as the ship pitched
propelled away from shore
toward the fettered horizon

VOYAGE

Life itself became disease
aboard the *Bell*, passage to Jamaica—
first landing in Kingston, my illness
at sea gave way to a greater unhinging,
the period they call here *the seasoning*.
For weeks I was adrift, mind
fretted with fevers, body wracked
with chills afflicting even the strongest
who breach these shores.
Brother, I was counted dead,
then nearly dead. When we arrived
and for many a time after,
I was nine parts, nine tenths
out of ten, stark staring mad.

ANOTHER LIFE

Douglas calls this place Ayr Mount,
remapping for Scotia the island.
But not even the Ayr of home casts
such alchemical light, every red
quickly turned to blood and rust.
What in man yokes us to the past?
What name could contain the history
of any tract of land? This promontory
facing the sea, backward casts its gaze
across the Rio Grande Valley, lifts
its eyes toward the Blue Mountains.
It has done so long before we came,
will do so well after we are dust,
while the Ayr I knew, another life,
corrodes inside of this one.

LANDSCAPE

In the grim sky a tempest is brewing.
I watch the children of affliction,
backs carved from the swell of these hills,
curved against the arc of the whip, their sweat
and blood rivering flesh. Machetes swing,
day in, day out, while the woe-delighted
minister of grief hovers above us all.
In this place, who and where am I
to be found? Home so hot, I'd thought
to give dodging and doubling. I winged
for the Atlantic, not seeking fortune,
the siren call for many a traveller,
but to flee disgrace. Now possessing
neither house nor hame, I am wanderer,
sojourner in this strange land, master
over some, slave to ill-begotten Fate,
to Douglas and his every command.
I, who wished to be a clever fellow,
to find a way free of the trappings
of a world so narrow, have entered one
yet more winnowed, have become
the detested Negro Driver I feared,
harrowed by the feeling of the damned.

DEAR GILBERT,

You cannot know what I have witnessed,
what I have done. Now this word
you send of my infant twins
gone to the grave, while faithless
Jean remains steadfast in reproach—
how much is one man to bear?
I did penance before the Kirk,
removed myself to earth
among these mountains, yet censure
and blame shadow my every step,
misery clings to the hem of my clothes.
Not you, brother, not anyone
could fathom the depths of my suffering,
the greater portion I've heaped
upon myself in this rash pursuit.
Of all that wrings the mind,
beyond compare the worst we owe
to guilt. In the store of torments,
there is no keener lash.

RIVER AYR

Wending in its winding,
nothing so fickle, unreliable
resides in us as conscience,
proving itself unworthy
of halting the course of passion.
In Alloway, the river ran
past the mill on its way to sea,
and I, a boy, wandered
to-and-fro along its banks.
Wending in its winding,
undeterred by rock or stone,
as the current surged, urged
the water forward, so I
flung myself into that force.

THE HOUR OF DREAM

In the space before dawn
something enters
wafting with wind
across the window's transom
in silvered light her sweet
sonsie face graces
my sleeping and
on waking she is
the sun settling trees
back into their rightful
selves on waking
she is all
that might obliterate
for a moment
the dark

DEAR GILBERT,

The novelty of a Poet
in my obscure situation has raised me
to some height. When talk turns to Slavery,
arguments for its brutal necessity
prevail, and I sit at the table of plenty,
bite back my tongue. Our men,
transplanted to rocky soil, struck
a Faustian bargain. How could they
turn against themselves? And I,
who find myself among the rubble,
am only a rhyming Mason, flatterer
seeking my name through poetry,
armament against my further ruin.
I was born to the class that labours.
I toil under this sun yet cannot meet
its lease. The few pounds I clear,
I submit to you, dear brother,
for those entrusted to my care.
I know full well I am insufficient
to this or any other earthly task.
Long having studied myself, I ken
pretty exactly what ground
I stand upon. In serving the Muse,
I have often forsaken the Life.

FOR PROMISED JOY

Suffer me to want her.
Suffer me to ask for nothing
but laughter, hers filling
the drafts and breathing
hollows of my room.
Each time she enters, suffer me
to be suffused in scent
of her, my eyes condemned
by sight of her. Suffer me
to ask love to dwell
in a place not meant
for love's habitation,
in vain to take
what is mine and not mine,
to theft from brutality beauty,
without hesitation, without
thought of consequence.
Suffer me to face love's cruelty
that knows no boundary.

BARD

On this island, distinction between
planter and bookkeeper wanes. Home,
or its ghost, binds us, an apparition
holding powerful sway. Bard,
they ask me to ferry Scotia
in tunes increasingly played
in drawing rooms from Port Antonio
to Kingston, salving exile's wounds.
Bard, in truth my name has made
a small noise across this island,
in Masonic halls, at Planters' balls.
My life's wish has only ever been
to make a song the equal to Nature,
to the stories of our heroic countrymen
who sheltered in every den and dell.
In Jamaica, if they bid me sing,
am I not all I ever wanted to be?

DOUGLAS'S REPLY

They are good for nothing but toiling and fucking.
Don't talk to me of the inalienable rights
of man. These are not men. The proof
of their brutish nature? Tell me: Who
of our lot could withstand such bestial labour
under this punishing sun? Who of our women
would squat in fields to give birth,
like the lowliest of animals, or take the whip
but be unbridled in bed? You've had
your taste of her, choosing to forget
from the start what was inevitable. You think
you are the first to be pricked by regret,
standing here, idiotically spouting of love?
Telling me you've taken the liberty, nae
the trouble, to write my brother? Good God,
you are more stupid, man, than even I
imagined. Of course he took pity on you.
My brother lives in the manner I secure for him
and wants to know nothing of the how,
the sacrifices exacted daily. My brother
believes he is good. And I let him. I am who
stops his fiction from fraying, who keeps
his whole damn world spinning.
Like so many of our countrymen
at a remove, he has turned soft and warms
to the notion these Africans have souls.
The prigs back home grow fatter and fatter
on sugar, never stepping foot on this island,
never knowing what the likes of you and I
endure. Yet they think they can legislate
to us what is right and wrong? *Now*,
when we are so far gone, *now* they are ready
to address the moral cause. Did you really
expect whatever reply my brother sent

to sway me? Womanish sentimentality
has always been your undoing, Burns. Lofty ideals
may find audience in drawing rooms
of the few. But ask yourself: what have idle
or even impassioned debates ever amounted to,
besides self-righteous piety? Better yet,
ask your drinking companions, for all this talk
of rights, what they do with their nights.
Where do you think these mulattoes and reds
running all about have come from, and what
exactly would happen to our way of life
were every mongrel and half-breed saved?
I ken the desire to do right by your family
back in Ayrshire—though by that measure
I'm afraid you've also missed the mark.
But to entertain or scheme to buy the wench
or this bairn you believe yours? That is right madness.
Burns, a way out you could not buy yourself.

DEAR GILBERT,

Darkness and Despair loiter,
training me in their sights. Once more,
I have been transported
by the thought I could say farewell
to the pain and weariness of life.
A hundred times I've wished
I could resign it as an officer
resigns commission. But this letter
from you has brought me back.
Our Mason brothers have taken up
the cause of this poor poet,
there is talk of a second printing.
Can it be true, the dream possible
in exile? That I might glimmer
into futurity? Or is it more madness
to think poverty and obscurity
are not my only path ahead, pride
again deceiving me, entreating me
believe I may be remembered
through my creations? These creatures
have long been my sole, my only
faithful companion, brother. Here,
as elsewhere, they are counterpoise
to a world I've never known
as anything but alien.

TAM O' SHANTER

In the wee hours returning from a Mason
gathering where I'd been bousing,
perchance the whiskey or wind and rain
that rose up round me howling muddled
my brain, but past and present agreed
to an exchange. I was carried over sea
back to Alloway, my horse and I passing
the auld Kirkyard, moving at such a pace
to gain the keystone of the bridge.
Something pursued us that night. I knew
not what exactly, but recalled evil spirits
cannot follow a body over water
and spurred my mare to full-frothed gallop,
till she brought us clattering across the river.
Zigzagging a path the rest of our journey,
we arrived once more at Springbank,
whence I set pen to page to recount the tale
I enclose, dear brother, the story of our hero
Tam and the fateful night he met with bogles
(duppies, here, being the same creature).
Poor Tam, on this misbegotten ride,
could nae tether time nor tide. Benighted
traveller, he was nae wise yet saw—
whatever danger may be in plunging
forward, there is ever more in turning back.

AUGUR

Recent unrest in Haiti, renewed fervour
for Abolition back home, give rise
to Douglas's widening spell of dread.
Awakening to the end encroaching,
he holds all at Springbank hostage
to his unpredictable, eruptible moods.
Mornings, making my way to the fields
I must pass the kitchen, and she is always
there, the child at her side uncommonly
fair and growing willful, all the more
like her mother, who senses my gaze
but will not countenance it. This act
of petition and refusal we replay,
as day gives way to day, and Douglas
sputters over a bit of errant flour or sugar,
tearing about in mindless rage.
Unmoving, she wields silence
in her body like an axe, her body
no longer yielding the sweetness
of the girl I knew. The other slaves
whisper of what she's turned into:
Obeah-woman claiming dominion
over life and death, crooking out
for herself and *that child* undue position
in the house. Jealousy is currency
amongst the slaves, yet in times of need
the girls and women have no choice
but to seek her. Douglas knows why
there are fewer and fewer births
each passing year. He hears the scuttling
chatter that augurs truth. But facing Nancy,
even he falls mute. Like all, he fiercely fears
whatever he cannot rule nor ken.

CRUMBO-JINGLE

Days fold into days and I hold fast
to snatches of heart-songs learnt
before the hearth when, a child,
I listened as my mother sang.
I carried those airs across the sea.
I bear them now, as more
and more I morph into another,
a spirit absented from its host.
Evenings I return to this room,
to shape memory to music
whilst night stretches without end,
taunting me to confront the rift
in myself. The crumbo-jingle, the poems
I send for safekeeping, these songs
I offer to the work of preservation,
so faithfully—could they salvage
my life? Could they recover our voices,
restore our better selves? They are all
I have and all that stays bedlam
from overtaking me. In time,
every man becomes the nightmare
from which he cannot wake. As the clock
strikes out the hour upon the hour.

FATE

Had my words been received at home
to greater acclaim, they may have
offered a way out. But for every man
time is tethered to a fate unwavering.
Master and slave alike are chained
on this island to cycles of too-much rain,
to drought and blight that ruin crops.
Each year, my health has worsened
in this clime, where I've seen men
far better than I fall to disease
of body and mind, spirit and soul.
And why have I been spared?
My weakened nerves disquiet
me and, for lengthening spells,
I am incapable of any good at all.
Deepening bouts of depression batter,
leaving me wasted and spent,
whilst Douglas, ever drunk, daily curses
this useless poet his brother sent,
this idiot loathe to use the whip.
He would've long ago returned me
were it not the blot, the stain I'd be
on his already bloodied ledger.
A monster of the highest order, Douglas.
Yet even he is unwilling to condemn
a fellow Scotsman to certain death.
And from the beginning, the end
was visible, already written—
I would not survive another crossing.

RISING

Day and night the mountains speak.
From distant fields, lit by fire, day and night
comes the drumming that will not cease,
fomenting fear in every planter, stirring
restlessness and desire amongst the slaves.
Nearly three decades have passed
since Tacky's rebellion failed and Nanny
now rumoured dead. Yet memory
survives, their spirits roaming these hills,
as the threat of the next rising gathers
like rain clouds on the horizon.
To incant the names of the dead
is to invite the charge of treason.
So silence becomes the cost
extracted from every man who labours
beneath the bootheel of history.
Dear brother, this letter will never
reach. Like so many thoughts of late,
they are as fragments of dream, thrashing
in my head. Or should I commit
even one rashly to the page, I would fast
tear that sheet to shreds, burn it
to cinder and ash. Soon enough I will
be called to account for my sins. So what
could it matter to confess them to you
or any other? Brother, what would I say
in truth, but I have borne witness to,
been reluctant participant in this madness.
I have watched as all of us are bound
by Fate, cruel twine ordained
not by any law of God or Nature,
but of this world we have designed.
This world, where profit is the first
and last word. Violence, both rule and reason.

SPRINGBANK

Place of memory now in ruin.
This point overlooking the sea,
this cliff, this perch, paradise
to none but one who came
imagining he could be lord, could be
unmoored from class and caste.
The way past is always the way
through. After sea, overland
we traversed mountain, rocky passages
flanking us, abutted by gullies,
oversized plants casting their shadows.
The horses' hooves trod and trod
until stone gave way to field,
and we entered the valley, approaching
the Great House from behind.
That first sight rises still in my mind,
bodying forth false promise.
Leuk twice or ye leap ance echoes,
now fruitless. O, what foolishness
lies in the heart of man, gleaming
wish to be more that waits
for its chance to pounce and savage.

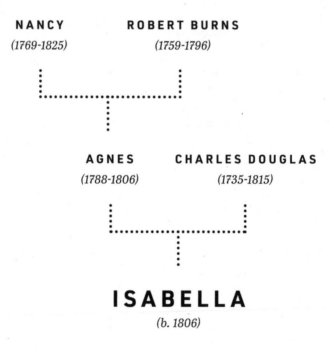

NANCY
(1769-1825)

ROBERT BURNS
(1759-1796)

AGNES
(1788-1806)

CHARLES DOUGLAS
(1735-1815)

ISABELLA
(b. 1806)

TUTU GBƆVI

Lullaby (Ewe, Ghana)

Tutu gbɔvi
Tutu gbɔvi
Nana* me le aʄea me o
Meke ola fa vi na
Ao dzedze vinye
Bɔnu bɔnu kpoo

DON'T CRY LITTLE CHILD

Lullaby (English rendering)

My dear one
My dear one
Your grand/mother* isn't home
Who are you crying for
Don't cry little child
Oh my dear one don't cry

*in Ewe, Nana means mother or grandmother

ISABELLA

SCOTLAND, 1825-26

Behold, I lay in Zion for a foundation a stone,
a tried stone, a precious cornerstone.

—ISAIAH

MEMORY

my first was sound

wielding an axe

rending flesh

torn from a throat

as a child rendered orphan

hungering to feed

the second was

but fire

lighting kitchen walls

from the sea's memory

tilling soil

not even rain

without end

we cross

stone

brought forth from her hands

severing the necks of fowl

from bone that sound

the cry she'd made

stolen across an ocean

ceaselessly to feed

no sound

kindled of her hands

dredging blood

blood

blood

that falls and falls

not any water

any riverbed

can absolve

THE BARD, EDINBURGH, 1825

Everywhere I turn, you ghost this city:
remnants in each drawing-room
conversation, your book of poems finding
too late your yearned-for fame, scores
of songs you composed in *exile* and returned
to *dear Scotia* now sung from every rafter.
Your spirit shadows each corridor
I turn down, as walking cobbled streets
I listen in echoes of my footfalls
for yours that never fell on these stones.
I work to piece together the man
she offered in snatches, not the legend
death has made you. But if not stitched
from story, where is the soul housed?
What is its right and lasting dwelling?
No doubt, you'd be pleased to see
they've erected a statue, your likeness
fronting Canongate Kirk, your back
fittingly turned from the grave.
Thirty years past your final breath
and biographers and critics circle,
feeding on your corpse, your life
churning an industry of myth.
And what could I say makes me
different from the rest? Haunting
library halls, frittering hours
in cloistered rooms, combing
scant recovered letters and your reclaimed
Springbank journal, I, your unclaimed kin,
asking words to perform the impossible:
to return the past whole. No,
truth be told, not whole but
the absence of you, that abscess in me.

STORY, THE FIRST

My father was an unexceptional man,
ordinary, *of his time*, as is said in defence
of men like him. My father, once possessed
perhaps of virtue, grew fou and foul-tempered,
his mind by avarice blunted and dulled.
He saw everything for the taking. And took.
Your daughter, my mother barely out of girlhood
when he began with her, was no exception.
In your time, you would have known him
as a younger, maybe better man, not
the mangled version I witnessed. My father
was unexceptional in every measure
but the one that mattered. His name
was Douglas, and in Jamaica that made him
laird. Fully of his time, he was all feared
true of men born of colony: wretchedness
is fast imprinted on them, their souls
shrunken by the whip, which seldom fails
to destroy not only those forced
to yield to it, but all who wield it.

SPRINGBANK

Was all the world I'd known.
A child there, I was hers, Miss Nancy's kin,
no matter this skin, these eyes belonging
to his face. *Your father could not*
look at you without seeing disgrace
was the only answer she'd relent to offer.
Even when her life waned, she would not
unlock the past, tell me what she'd said
that made him let us go, why he paid
and paid to send us away and away.
We left first for Kingston, and a door
closed behind us, a door
I was never meant to open again.
In Kingston, my grandmother was passed off
as my slave. By the time our ship docked
in Greenock, she was my servant, and we
threaded into a tale, so tightly
woven, no one would guess my origin.
What she sacrificed was everything
of herself to see me freed. But my father?
You kent him and his world so intimately
what I've surmised will be no surprise.
What Douglas understood was expedience.
I was simply evidence. I needed to be erased.

WOMAN IN AN EDINBURGH DRAWING ROOM

I kent your father. From Ayrshire,
the Douglases. I knew it straight away
when I glimpsed you. You're the dead
stamp of his mother, though a shade
tawnier I'd say, no doubt on account
of your early dousing in sun. Still,
I'm sure you've heard you favour
the Douglas side many a time,
especially back in Glasgow, no?
Och, but what a tragedy, your father's
untimely, violent end. It's just dreadful
what's going on all over noo. To be sure,
slavery is a terrible, terrible thing.
But the ruin of more and more merchants—
'tis a disgrace, aye? You must be grateful
to be here, what with the right madness
of the world these days. But listen to me,
blethering on about such unpleasant business.
Your husband is a saviour, surely you know.
When my daughter took ill this winter,
I don't ken what we would have done
without him. He's a braw doctor and man,
your husband. I hear you married just this year.
Aye, I expect wee ones should soon be along.

HUSBAND,

If you knew me

    would you see me

or would you fail

    me fail to take me

whole and not

    in slivers given

not shards

    of story told

and told till even I

    could forget

there was another

    a girl who stood

before this woman

    who robed herself

in myths of nation

    purity fealty

demanded of her

    so now

could I breathe

    her back now

could I begin again

    to unclothe her

strip myself

    from under her flesh

how would she

    speak

to stitch

    a different tale

what risk

PASSING

You are wondering how I did this.
It was easier than you might imagine.
Of course Douglas too knew it would be,
how quickly I could be made to disappear,
how deftly the eye deceives. At first
I was afraid, concealing myself
in plain sight. But by and by, I grew aware
people see what they want, content
to make my body a map, to chart
any history they desired. If queried further,
I'd recite the tale we'd rehearsed.
My mother was a Spaniard, over
from the neighbouring island of Cuba—
my name, your sister's I'd been given,
conveniently aiding the ruse. And so the yarn
was spun: my mother and father meeting
at a planter's ball, a whirlwind courtship,
a marriage, and never was she to return
to her island or true home in Spain,
dying in exile, birthing me. It was a fairy tale
of a faraway place, resplendent
with the necessary, beautiful, tragic
ending: the death of my mother,
the exchange of one life for another.
That much at least was true.
At first when we came to Glasgow,
facing the gaggle of girls at school,
I had to be careful. They could trap me
with their incessant curiosity, begging me
to say words the odd way to their ears
I did, or beseeching me comb my hair,
so tightly coiled compared to theirs,
as if I were a doll and we were playing
an elabourate game of dress-up.

I had to rehearse my part, to never mistake
the secrets girls offer one another for safety,
to never let my disguise slip. But soon,
it grew to be my second skin. I grew
so comfortable in the lies, in the lying,
I could believe the sound of my own voice,
and memory began to give way
bit by bit to fiction. And the Douglases,
here in Scotland, they knew all this
and wanted nothing to do with it, with me,
grateful he'd left us just far enough
from Ayrshire, with just enough
of a purse for our silence
to be bought. And it was, for a long time,
easier than you could imagine. Here,
people know so little of the truth
of the colonies that fill their coffers,
if even they imagine Jamaica,
it is an abject paradise or prison.
In their minds, in their vision,
where I'm from is a geographical invention
entirely of their making. So, everything
I tell them, in their compassion,
in their hubris, they believe.

CHANCE

But there was a man of late who saw me, one
Zachary Macaulay. Like you, he fled Scotland
trying to outrun the ruin he'd made of his life.
Unlike you, he returned to tell the story
of what in Jamaica he'd seen and become.
My husband insisted we hear him speak.
How could a man be fighting for the rights
of Negroes who'd been himself a slaver?
Surely we must care to hear his appeals?
How could I say no? We were there,
as chance would have it, in London the night.
And, after the talk, my husband again insisted,
We must stay to meet this great man, Macaulay.
You may of course guess what happened next.
It was as if I were flayed by his gaze,
peering into and through me. I knew he knew.
Yet all the while we three kept chattering on,
my husband mainly, laughing and smiling,
holding up the inane custom of sharing
pleasantries, despite the horrors Macaulay
had recounted, the intimate details of a place,
a time, I thought I'd left behind. All, while
Macaulay's eyes kept unmasking me.
And then, it was over, and I back in this body,
being led by my husband, whisked out
into the cold and passing the windows
of the library, that space where moments before
we'd been standing still illuminated but darkening
the glass outside, rendering it incapable
of reflecting back to us ourselves.

HUSBAND,

For all the faith in argument in principle in reason

for all the books you hand me bid me read

for all in the dark I pretend

for all the pursuit of equality of righteousness and good

for all the rights of man the vindication of woman

for all in the dark I pretend we are

for all the moral cause abolition the struggle for freedom

for all in the dark I pretend we are just

for all the history of heroes and foes the victors and the vanquished

for all the talk and talk and talk

for all in the dark I pretend we are just one soul

what would it mean to see

not Love not Truth not Beauty but who

has been in your house who sleeping in your bed?

AE FOND KISS

become Nancy

    when thieved to Jamaica

you made her

    your Muse immortal

in your paean to love

    and parting from the start

she must have seen

    the severing

was inevitable

    must have known

dark despair

    would always benight

must have heard

    beneath your words

what words

    in that place never

could be coaxed

    to sing if ever

you loved her

    what did your love

for her mean

    what use to her

your tears

    pledged your sighs

waged in vain

    in the end

who paid

    best and dearest

I ask you

    in the end

for whom

    did fortune grieve

HUSBAND, THE TRUTH IS

my mother was every sound

stripped from silence

my father the figure

lurching through dreams

in the carrion of history

I am dismantled reassembled

dismantled

and not you could save me

not anyone could save me

from the truth

in this carrion history

I was born

without purchase born

of rape thereafter

what could I be

what could my body be

but ransom

INHERITANCE

my grandmother taught me

to fear the sea

she crossed first as a girl

on that passage

her mother's voice

lost her language

lost each lullaby

swallowed by the sea's

cavernous din

the roiling

waves she'd meet

again and again in dreams

moaning thrashing

waking years later

urging me each time

remember

with every surface

what lies beneath

in journeying here

what choice was I given

but to morph

shape-shifting to what she feared

in learning to be

more of you more

like you mimicking

your speech your dress lacing

myself invisibly

into your world a shadow

passing seamlessly

through your cosseted rooms

walking dusk-lit streets

no one I see knowing

her name but yours

everywhere everywhere

how have I not betrayed

                     her in death my life

erasing and erasing her

IN THE FIELD

lies the shipwrecked ship
broken mast and riggings
resembling an angel or bird fallen
from a high place wings splayed feathers
like a halo of the body in the field
I wander the body of night
bereft of sight or made bereft by sight
of this vessel stranded in a clearing
never meant to hold its form
unable to conjure the shape
of longing every ship contains
in this dream of the field
I am the absence of ship
its hollowed-out hull the waves
the voices of the drowned
beating against my ribs
and I cannot stop the cries
and I cannot unstopper my ears
as all night comes the tolling
why have you survived if not for this?

TO A MOUSE

All your life you feared the pack
would snuff your scent. But at the end,
there was only Nancy, hers the breath
grazing your neck, hers the arms
laying you down. And you saw,
in a flash of final sight some are gifted,
the weight of the choice you'd made:
how your love had increased
her portion of cruelty. Then,
your silence was the silence
of regret. This is the debt, the one
you could have paid, I want tendered.
This is how I want to envision your life
flickering out. But my wanting
is never enough. Your words
forsake us both. I've searched them,
time and again, to arrive back where I began.
For ten years in Jamaica, you mourned
your unsung genius most. Ten years
ambition rotted you, and you tipped your ear
away from her toward Scotland,
distant music you husbanded,
whittled, wagering everything
on the past, as if its recovery
could compensate the present. And I,
in this present you failed so utterly
to imagine, how do I not retrod
the stones of your selfsame path? How
do I claim you as kin and bear knowing—
even you, who glimpsed divinity
in the smallest of creatures, lit
the animal soul, spoke
nothing of her suffering?

AT THE HOUR OF DUPPY AND DREAM, MISS NANCY SPEAKS

You think what lies before you
asks more than you can bear
but I am with you now as I was
when you came into this world
your one eye looking forward
the other forever looking back
from the netherworld
you were flung into this one
squalling full of that scent
we could not wash away
your mother's breath extinguished
as you gulped your first
the caul swaddling your face
till we lifted it unveiling
beholding the unasked-for
girl-child cast down
in a place of stone
of men who cannot see to see
do not hear what needs listening
men who have riven
borders and nations and you
in whom the rift has opened
hear me for I was there
in the beginning
witness as you entered
as you came dusking
tearing all asunder rending
the fabric they call Truth

HOLYROOD, 1826

Spring again, and the hills are lit with gorse.
Each day I walk from the city's centre,
leave behind its cobblestones, the closes'
stink, the everywhere grey of brick on brick,
to take in this yellow flowering, its profusion
like the poui of my childhood, unfettered.
I climb rocky paths to the Abbey's ruins,
from whose heights I peer through
windowless rooms, out to sea. Here,
the past silts the present, salts air.
How many times have I made this ascent?
How many must I make it more,
searching the horizon, scouring clouds
for signs of how they lived and died,
trying to read truthfully my inheritance,
what now I am meant to pass on?
No longer a girl, it is time I turn from all
the given names to learn what land knows:
how forged in fire hills are birthed,
how loch and sky and sea converge
inside the eye's trickery. No longer a child,
I must find a way to stand in this place,
and every other, not earthed for me.

THE CHOICE

who made my mind unfit

for what I'm told

is my soul's true nature

if half-mad

half-fed what idea

yet be planted in my brain

by what if any gods there be

the Truth

I find in books not written

with glimmer of me

is one she owned her life

made writ Freedom

cannot be gifted

you by another

when there is no choice

there is still choice

forgive me my trespasses

my past this present

forgive me all my ancestors

our history forgive me

husband but love

is nothing if it is not

a mirror for us to gaze

into our razored selves

and I can be no longer

hushed nor still

without sound

when phantoms

keep ringing round

my life must be

outwith my own

must speak in some measure

for her and all who are

still yoked

for as long as smoke

                              is wreathing

the fields the fields

                              still burning

VOYAGE

For days, our ship had listed in storms,
but at last the waters stilled.
In the middle of our crossing
came a calm, and the sea,
a sheet of glass, reflected only
moon and stars and cloudless sky,
as if all that was before and all
that was to come was dream.
Above and below us
lay two firmaments, and we,
marooned by history, by memory,
became the between.
In the wake of tempests, the sea
offered faint reckoning, wave
upon wave dimly echoing
wind's lashing of rope to mast,
as that night splintered
into every night. And the stars,
numberless as the souls lost
to the sea's depths, revealed
the routes we would have to take
to recover the wreckage of ourselves.

THE PROPHET AND GOD'S COMPLAINT

All is echo and repetition.
All is echo and repetition.
All is echo and repetition.

NO RUINED STONE

May 2018: for my grandmother

When the dead return
they will come to you in dream
and in waking, will be the bird
knocking, knocking against glass, seeking
a way in, will masquerade
as the wind, its voice made audible
by the tongues of leaves, greedily
lapping, as the waves' self-made fugue
is a turning and returning, the dead
will not then nor ever again
desert you, their unrest
will be the coat cloaking you,
the farther you journey
from them the more
distance will maw in you,
time and place gulching
when the dead return to demand
accounting, wanting
and wanting and wanting
everything you have to give and nothing
will quench or unhunger them
as they take all you make as offering.
Then tell you to begin again.

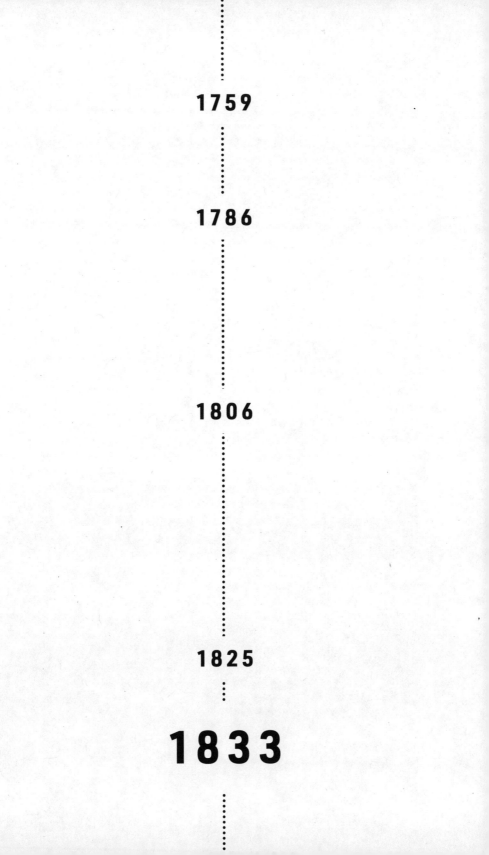

1759

1786

1806

1825

1833

AUTHOR'S NOTE

The best laid schemes o' Mice an' Men
Gang aft agley,
An' lea'e us nought but grief an' pain,
for promis'd joy!
— R O B E R T   B U R N S

From Ayrshire in the Lowlands of Scotland, Robert Burns is arguably the most well-known Scot. His literary work survived the brief span of his life (1759-1796) and is beloved to the present day in Scotland and around the world. The myth of the "Ploughman Poet" is also alive and well over two hundred years after his death. Burns seems to have had a strong hand in constructing this image of himself: the self-taught, working-class man of letters who flourished in inhospitable soil to become a literary genius. Like many of the stories of famous men, this one persists, even in the face of facts that would ask us to reckon with a far more complex version of Burns' life.

In the winter of 2015, on my first visit to Scotland, I learned a lesser-known story of the Bard: late in the summer of 1786, Burns had made plans to emigrate from Scotland. He was going to work as a bookkeeper on a slave plantation in Jamaica, in the employ of brothers who also hailed from Ayrshire, Charles and Patrick Douglas. The Douglases owned two plantations on the island's north coast, in and near Port Antonio, from the late 18th to early 19th century. The larger of the two plantations, Ayr Mount—Springbank being the name of the Great

House on the plantation and used interchangeably to refer to the plantation—was where Burns was destined. "Bookkeeper," in application to the work Burns would have done on the plantation, is a misnomer. Had he gone to Jamaica, he would have been directly involved in the operation of the plantation, responsible for overseeing and managing the work performed by enslaved Africans.

There has been in Scotland a longstanding tendency to ascribe West Indian slavery entirely to the English, though in the last twenty years this has begun to change. It's well documented by historians and other researchers of the 18th century that many of the "merchants" in and around Glasgow trafficked in and amassed huge profits from the slave trade. By the late 18th century, over a third of the whites in Jamaica were Scottish, and Scots owned 30% of the plantations and 32% of enslaved Africans on the island. Jamaica was the most valuable British colony during slavery, producing the greatest wealth for individual plantation owners and building the Empire. It was also the most brutal colony, and on Scots-owned Jamaican plantations the survival rate for Africans was the lowest across the island: less than four years upon arrival.

Throughout the late summer and into the fall of 1786, Burns booked passage on three different vessels that sailed from Scotland to Jamaica. There is relatively little commentary from Burns on this plan. Staunch advocate for the "rights of man," as evinced by his prose and poems, Burns was not an Abolitionist, though he would undoubtedly have been aware of the movement, which gained traction in Scotland in the late 18th century. The highly public case in 1777 of Joseph Knight, a Jamaican slave brought to Scotland by his owner John Wedderburn, whom Knight sued for his freedom, was a watershed moment. The case declared that slavery was not recognised by Scots' law and made slaveholding illegal in Scotland, though it did not abolish it in the colonies. Abolition of slavery would not occur in the British Caribbean for more than fifty years after the Knight case, in 1833—still three decades prior to the United States in 1865.

Over the course of his life, Burns was well-versed in international affairs and politics and influenced by Enlightenment thinking and the events of the French and American Revolutions. But on the subject of slavery, he remained largely silent. In his journals and letters, there's one notable but brief discussion of his plan to become a "Negro Driver." In his poems and songs, there are a few mentions of slavery, though in figurative and often highly sentimental terms. All this makes it difficult if not impossible for biographers and scholars in the present to definitively answer the question: why would Scotland's great Bard, a man who in his work passionately espoused liberty, have been apparently so ready to involve himself in an institution that categorically denied other human beings their liberty?

Based on circumstantial evidence, most can only conjecture. The prevailing view is that Burns' decision to flee to Jamaica was an ill-begotten plan, an act of desperation. In the late summer of 1786, he was facing financial ruin and trying to extricate himself from a series of bad love affairs, including possibly with "Highland Mary" and definitely with Jean Armour, a young woman of Ayrshire, who at the time was pregnant out of wedlock with twins by Burns. Jean Armour was one of a number of women with whom Burns had liaisons and children over the course of his life, but she was the only one—after a protracted, complicated relationship—he ultimately married.

As fate would have it, Burns' book of poems sold out its first run in a matter of weeks upon its release in 1786. This allowed him to delay sailing for Jamaica on the ship he'd first booked passage, the *Nancy*—ironically also the name of the beloved of one of Burns's most famous and enduring songs, "Ae Fond Kiss." After the *Nancy* sailed without him, he then, however, continued to pursue plans to migrate and booked passage on two subsequent ships bound for Jamaica, the *Bell* and the *Roselle*, neither of which he ultimately boarded. The success of his book appears to have been a major factor in Burns' decision to remain in Scotland, to seek to further his literary fortune at home. By the close of 1786, he was pursuing a second printing for his book and had abandoned his plan to emigrate altogether.

Over the course of the last ten years of his life, Burns wrote a handful of additional poems, expanding his sole volume of poetry, *Poems, Chiefly in the Scottish Dialect*. During his lifetime, the book was reprinted and received strong and favourable attention at home and abroad. Burns' greatest literary output in the last decade of his life, though, came in the form of hundreds of songs he collected and wrote, while farming and then working as a government official, an Exciseman, in Ayrshire. His songs comprised the vast majority of those gathered into two major collections of traditional Scots music, *Scots Musical Museum* and *A Select Collection of Original Scottish Airs for the Voice*, brought out in turn by editors James Johnson and George Thomson.

While Burns struggled financially throughout his entire life, for his work on these song collections, he refused payment. For Burns, the writing of songs and poems—*crumbo-jingle*—was his self-professed avocation. All his life, Burns was beset not only by financial difficulties but by poor health. From our contemporary medical vantage point, Burns appears to have suffered from rheumatic and heart disorders and debilitating mental illness, experiencing major depressive episodes across his life. Robert Burns died in 1796, likely of heart failure, at the age of 37.

In writing this book, I took my cues from Burns' life and work. But the resulting poems and the characters of Burns and Douglas and their relations and descendants as conceived are works of imagination and speculative history. The poems offer an account of an alternate past, given voice primarily by a fictive Burns and his fictional granddaughter, a white-skinned black woman, a mulatta who is "passing."

I wrote this book neither to condemn Burns on the count of slavery nor to exonerate him. I wrote these poems neither to account for the story of Jamaica and Scotland nor my own or my family's story. But this book is not *not* about all of these—and our responsibility to the past, our inheritance, and the choices we face and make as individuals given the circumscription of our lives by history.

Jamaica, the country I'm from, resulted from the tectonic meeting of the Americas, Africa, and Europe. I am of that story of rupture and new birth. In retrospect, once I learned how nearly Burns had come to migrating to Jamaica and being imbricated in slavery, perhaps the question that entered my mind and took up residence there is not altogether surprising.

What surprised me is that it was a question to which I felt compelled to ask poetry to respond. Doing so led me farther afield than any book of poems I'd written prior—to archives and travels in Scotland and Jamaica, to the pages of biography and literary and cultural history, to meetings with scholars, writers, artists, and Burns' aficionados—yet returned me with full force to some of my earliest obsessions and vexations, including with Romantic poetry and the Enlightenment's ideals and occlusions, with absent fathers, mothers, and countries, with migration, exile, and memory. Following the first question often led me only to more of its kind. That instigator was like a sore in the mouth my tongue kept seeking.

What would have happened had he gone?

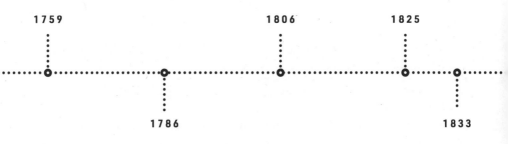

1759   1806   1825

1786   1833

TIMELINE

Of events in *No Ruined Stone* and in the historical record.
When events occur <u>only</u> in *No Ruined Stone*, they appear on the right.

JANUARY 25, 1759
Robert Burns born in Alloway, Scotland, eldest son of William Burnes and Agnes Broun. He will grow up receiving a classical education, privately tutored, while farming in Ayrshire.

SUMMER 1781
Burns experiences first major depressive episode while away from his family in the town of Irvine.

1784
Burns' father dies, leaving Burns and his brother Gilbert responsible for the family farm in Ayrshire and the care of their mother and siblings.

1785
Burns' first child born out of wedlock. Her mother Elizabeth Patton is a servant on the family farm. Elizabeth (the name also of the child) will be raised by Burns' mother on the farm. While Elizabeth is pregnant, Burns meets and begins a relationship with Jean Armour, six years his junior. Burns' younger brother John also dies in this same year.

In Jamaica, a major hurricane devastates Port Antonio.

EARLY IN 1786

Jean Armour is pregnant with Burns' twins out of wedlock, while Burns is having an affair with Mary Campbell ("Highland Mary").

SUMMER 1786

Burns is arranging for the publication of his first book while performing his third public penance for "the sin of fornication," the family farm is failing, and Burns learns that Jean's father plans to sue him. Burns decides to migrate and begins arrangements. He accepts employment as a Bookkeeper on the Douglas plantation and books passage to sail for Jamaica.

JULY 31, 1786

Burns' book, *Poems, Chiefly in the Scottish Dialect* (Kilmarnok edition), is published.

SEPTEMBER 3, 1786

Jean Armour gives birth to Burns' twins.

SEPTEMBER 1786

Burns boards the *Bell*, bound for Jamaica.

OCTOBER 1786

Mary Campbell ("Highland Mary") dies.

OCTOBER 1786

Burns' twins by Jean Armour die.

LATE IN 1786

Burns arrives at Springbank, Ayr Mount plantation in Port Antonio, Jamaica. Charles Douglas is "Master" of the plantation, co-owner with his brother, Patrick, back home in Scotland. The Douglases, like Burns, hail from Ayrshire.

1787

Burns begins a many year relationship with Nancy, an enslaved African woman at Springbank, ten years his junior.

Agnes, daughter of Burns and Nancy, is born into slavery.

1790

Burns is in bad health and again severely depressed. Yet he continues to write and, in November 1790, writes one of his most famous poems, "Tam O' Shanter." He will continue writing poems and songs, contributing work to two collections of traditional Scottish songs, up until his death.

1793

The first volume of Thomson's *A Select Collection of Original Scottish Airs for the Voice*, a series to which Burns contributes a significant number of songs, is published.

1795

Second Maroon War in Jamaica occurs. During the eight-months conflict, martial law is instituted for periods across the island. The war ends with the signing of another treaty between the Maroons of Jamaica and the British, representing significant defeat this time for the Maroons and major concessions, including the Maroons' (renewed) agreement to return runaway slaves.

JULY 21, 1796
Robert Burns dies.

1797

The first volume of Johnson's *Scots Musical Museum* is published. Burns' contribution to the series, as with the one edited by Thomson, is significant.

1797

Poems, Chiefly in the Scottish Dialect, the expanded edition, is posthumously published in Edinburgh (in actual history, later editions appeared beginning in 1787). With it, critical attention to Burns' poems, songs, journals, letters, and to his life begins (in actual history, all this began in 1786, when *Poems, Chiefly in the Scottish Dialect* was first published).

1798

Cuffee, a Jamaican slave, escapes from a plantation in the western part of the island and forms a community in Cockpit Country, in the mountainous interior. Cuffee and his community will successfully resist slavery, provide safe haven for other runaway slaves, and elude recapture.

JULY 21, 1801
The first "Burns supper" takes place, on the fifth anniversary of his death, in Ayrshire. "Burns suppers" will be moved to the anniversary of his birth January 25th and take place annually not only in Scotland but around the world.

1806
Isabella is born into slavery at Springbank, Ayr Mount.
Isabella is the daughter of Agnes and Charles Douglas
and the granddaughter of Nancy and Robert Burns.
Isabella's mother, Agnes, dies in childbirth.

MAY 1, 1807
The Slave Trade Act of 1807 abolishes the British slave trade but does not abolish slavery.

1815
Isabella and her grandmother Nancy emigrate
from Jamaica to Glasgow, Scotland.

1815
Charles Douglas dies at Springbank, Ayr Mount in Port Antonio, Jamaica.

1822
The Anti-Slavery Society is founded in Glasgow, Scotland. Glasgow is known as one of the staunchest Abolitionist cities in Britain. Scotsman Zachary Macaulay, who had worked as a Bookkeeper from 1784-1789 on a plantation in Jamaica, is a leading voice and figure in the Anti-Slavery movement.

1825
Isabella marries and moves to Edinburgh.
Her grandmother Nancy dies the same year.

1833
Slavery in the British West Indies will be abolished.

ACKNOWLEDGMENTS

My sincere gratitude to Tyler Mills and Brianna Noll, Sven Birkerts and Bill Pierce, Geoffrey Brock, David Barber, Alex Houen and Adam Piette, Jessica Rogen, Sam Tongue, Jenny Molberg, Keetje Kuipers and Aaron Barrell, Rick Barot and Carolyn Kuebler, Jessica Faust, and John Whale, editors of the following magazines and journals in the US, England, and Scotland, in which poems in this collection first appeared, sometimes in earlier versions:

The Account, Agni, The Arkansas International, The Atlantic, Blackbox Manifold, Boulevard, Glasgow Review of Books, Pleaides, Poetry Northwest, New England Review, The Southern Review, Stand.

"No Ruined Stone" (You saturate the sight) was written in response to Calum Colvin's "Portrait of Hugh MacDiarmid" and was part of the 2018 Annual Exhibition of the Royal Scottish Academy of Art and Architecture, focused on linkages between poetry and visual art.

"No Ruined Stone" (When the dead return) was published in the Poem-a-Day project of the Academy of American Poets. Thank you to editor Evie Shockley.

"No Ruined Stone" (When the dead return) was translated into Spanish by Adalber Salas Hernández and appeared in *Jámpster* (Chile).

Several poems from this collection were published in *La Historia es un cuarto/History is a Room*, an anthology of my poems in Spanish, selected and translated by Adalber Salas Hernández (Mantis Editores, Mexico, 2021). For his own poetry, his translations, and our conversations, *un millón de gracias*.

Thank you to my editor Carey Salerno, for her unwavering faith and for seeing this book and me so clearly, and to Alyssa Neptune and everyone at Alice James Books for their tireless work.

There are numerous poets whose works informed my writing of this book, many long before I'd even conceived of this collection. I would never be able to name them all, but there is one I must single out. My deepest gratitude goes to Robert Burns, for his indelible work. My conversations with his poems, songs, journals, and letters and fragments of the same appear throughout this collection.

While researching this book, I was provided tangible and intangible measures of support by many individuals. Given the years I worked on this book, the list is long but I am sure still incomplete and any omissions are inadvertent.

In Jamaica, *nuff* thanks to: Eddie Baugh, Jennifer Brittan, Michael Bucknor, the late Victor Chang, Carolyn Cooper, Mervyn Morris, Rachel Moseley-Wood, Opal Palmer Adisa, Velma Pollard, James Robertson, Kimberly Robinson-Walcott, Isis Semaj-Hall, and Tanya Shirley—all at the University of the West Indies—Tanya Batson-Savage, Justine Henzell, Ann-Margaret Lim, Winsome Monica Minott, and Helen Morris. Each of them, in various ways and at various stages, offered meaningful encouragement with this project and the example of their own work. Particular thanks to Thera Edwards, at the University of the West Indies, for spending an afternoon pulling out maps and helping me see the past as written on the land and for later sending numerous digitized images and firsthand accounts of the natural and civic history of Jamaica from the late 18th century and early 19th century, all of which was invaluable to me in imagining my way back to Springbank. I'm grateful as well for my family and friends in Jamaica, who welcome me home each time I return. Special thanks to my sister Reneé for making space in her home and life in Kingston for me and for accompanying me to Port Antonio to face the ghosts of the past, my own and those that populate this book.

In Scotland, across several trips I made between 2015 and 2018, many people listened as I talked through my ideas, entertained my questions, and shared their knowledge and perspective, often pointing me in the direction of books I needed to read and places I needed to go. For their own artistic/scholarly/curatorial work and for helping me to see Burns and Scotland, *monie* a thanks to: Jane Brown at the Globe Inn in Dumfries; Stuart Cochrane at Ellisland Museum and Farm in Dumfries; Gerry Carruthers at the Centre for Burns Studies at the University of Glasgow; Robert Crawford at the University of St. Andrews; Graham Fagen, Glaswegian artist; Naomi Hare, artist and shopkeeper in Edinburgh; Colin Herd at the University of Glasgow; Asif Khan at the Scottish Poetry Library in Edinburgh; Nigel Leask at the Centre for Burns Studies at the University of Glasgow; Eleanor Livingstone of the StAnza Poetry Festival; Kirsteen McCue at the Centre for Burns Studies at the University of Glasgow; Jane McKie at the University of Edinburgh; Donnie Nicolson, driver in Inverness; Dilys Rose at the University of Edinburgh; Donnie Smith at the Scottish Storytelling Centre in Edinburgh; Alan Spence, Edinburgh Makar; Randall Stevenson at the University of Edinburgh; Chris Waddell at the Burns Birthplace Museum in Alloway; Jennifer Williams, poet in Edinburgh; and Duggie Young, driver on the Isle of Skye. Special thanks to: Calum Colvin, for his inimitable art, which informed and is part of this book, and for our spirited discussions about Burns, politics, history, and making art—and for conversation and collaboration yet to come; to Elizabeth Reeder and Amanda Thompson, for their powerful work as writers/artists and for opening their home to me and teaching me the beauty of a wee bit of whiskey on a cold night; to Rab Wilson, for his ethical and moving poems that come out of a life lived with conviction, and for taking me on the most extraordinary 'Burns tour' of Ayrshire, one that allowed me to see Burns and the world that made him in a way no amount of reading or visiting sites on my own could have equaled; and to Rab again and his wife Margaret, for the meals, poetry and song, and friendship—for inviting me into their *hame* when I arrived on their doorstep with nary a clue what I was doing. To all those in Scotland who welcomed this stranger *stravaiging* in your country, I remain in your debt.

Thank you to my department head and dean at Penn State and the provost at Bucknell prior, for funding the travel that enabled me to conduct some of my research for this book. Thank you to my colleagues and students, past and present, whose commitment to making art and to intellectual pursuit inspire me.

In addition to the poets already mentioned, thank you to: Elizabeth Alexander, EG Asher, Jacqueline Bishop, Paula Closson Buck, Vahni Capildeo, Kwame Dawes, Toi Derricotte, Camille Dungy, Cornelius Eady, Sonia Farmer, Danielle Legros Georges, Terrance Hayes, Katie Hays, Julia Kasdorf, Loretta Collins Klobah, Mia Leonin, Lieke Marsman, Adrian Matejka, Kei Miller, Tyler Mills, Rooja Mohassessy, Mihaela Moscaliuc, Shivanee Ramlochan, Lauren Russell, Chet'la Sebree, Tim Seibles, Charif Shanahan, Evie Shockley, Safiya Sinclair, Natasha Trethewey, Michael Waters, and Afaa Weaver. My conversations with your poems/ with each of you made this book better. Special thanks to Mia, Julia, and Chet'la, for reading the manuscript and fielding my questions with such care.

Last but farthest from least, thank you as always to my husband Steve, for being with me through the writing of this book from start to finish—listening to me hash out the project, pushing me to question what I was doing, making it possible for me to leave our home for the research this book required, and reading the manuscript with insight and gentleness. Thank you to our daughters, Rachel and Naomi: I am lucky to be your mother; you are both more wondrous, more beautiful, than any poem. And thank you to all my family and friends, near and far, in this world and otherwise: you know who you are. My love and gratitude for each of you knows no bounds.

BIBLIOGRAPHY

While working on this book, I referenced many sources and leaned heavily on the work of other scholars and artists who have gone before me. A selection of the texts I consulted is listed on the pages that follow.

I also visited and viewed archival materials, paintings, and exhibits at universities, museums, libraries, and other sites across Scotland and Jamaica. Two manuscripts of note: the *Glenriddle Manuscript* by Robert Burns and the *Jamaica Manuscript of Sugar Estates*, housed respectively in the archives of the National Library of Scotland in Edinburgh and the National Library of Jamaica in Kingston.

Crucial for me was hearing the songs of Robert Burns brought to life. I listened on repeat to the album, Eddi Reader *Sings the Songs of Robert Burns*. Very helpful, as well, were Burns' songs rendered by singers commissioned for *Editing Robert Burns for the 21st Century*, an online project of the Centre for Robert Burns Studies at the University of Glasgow that offers a wealth of resources on the Bard; Ghetto Priest's version of "The Slave's Lament"; Brina's version of "The Slave's Lament" (featuring Addis Pablo) and "Warmongerers by Name" (based on "Ye Jacobites by Name"); and Ken Boothe's version of "Green Grow the Rashes, O." These last three are part of a project produced by Kieran C. Murray titled, *Jamaica Sings Burns*.

Kamau Brathwaite, *The Development of Creole Society in Jamaica, 1770-1820*

Patrick Browne, *The Civil and Natural History of Jamaica*

Robert Burns, *Poems, Chiefly in the Scottish Dialect*

Robert Burns, *The Letters of Robert Burns*

Mavis C. Campbell, *The Maroons of Jamaica 1655-1796*

Gerard Carruthers, editor, *The Edinburgh Companion to Robert Burns*

Gerard Carruthers and Johnny Rodger, editors, *Fickle Man: Robert Burns in the 21st Century*

Catherine Carswell, *The Life of Robert Burns*

Robert Crawford, *The Bard: Robert Burns: A Biography*

Robert Crawford, editor, *The Best Laid Schemes: Selected Poetry & Prose of Robert Burns*

T.M. Devine, editor, *Recovering Scotland's Slavery Past: The Caribbean Connection*

Eric J. Graham, *Burns & the Sugar Plantocracy of Ayrshire*

Douglas Hall, *In Miserable Slavery: Thomas Thistlewood in Jamaica: 1750-1786*

Douglas Hamilton, *Scotland, the Caribbean and the Atlantic World, 1750-1820*

Allyson Hobbs, *A Chosen Exile: A History of Racial Passing in American Life*

Kay Redfield Jamison, *Touched with Fire: Manic-Depressive Illness and the Artistic Temperament*

Alan Karras, *Sojourners in the Sun: Scottish Migrants in Jamaica and the Chesapeake, 1740-1800*

Nigel Leask, editor, *The Oxford Edition of the Works of Robert Burns, v. 1, Commonplace Books, Tour Journals, and Miscellaneous Prose*

Nigel Leask, *Robert Burns & Pastoral: Poetry and Improvement in Late Eighteenth-Century Scotland*

Iain McCalman, editor, *The Horrors of Slavery and Other Writings by Robert Wedderburn*

Kirsteen McCue, *The Oxford Edition of the Works of Robert Burns, v. 4, Songs for George Thomson*

Hugh MacDiarmid, *Burns Today and Tomorrow*

James Mackay, *Burns: A Biography of Robert Burns*

Carol McGuirk, editor, *Critical Essays on Robert Burns*

Michael Morris, *Scotland and the Caribbean, c. 1740-1833: Atlantic Archipelagos*

Tom Normand, *Calum Colvin's Ossian: Fragments of Ancient Poetry*

Murray Pittock, *The Oxford Edition of the Works of Robert Burns, v. 2 & 3, Scots Musical Museum*

Geoff Palmer, *The Enlightenment Abolished: Citizens of Britishness*

Robert Renny, *An History of Jamaica*

James Robertson, *Joseph Knight*

Mary Seacole, *Wonderful Adventures of Mrs. Seacole in Many Lands*

G. Gregory Smith, *Scottish Literature: Character & Influence*

George F. Timpson, *Jamaican Interlude*

Amanda Thomson, *A Scots Dictionary of Nature*

J. R. Ward, *British West Indian Slavery, 1750-1834: The Process of Amelioration*

Cyric Williams, *A Tour through the Island of Jamaica from the Western to the Eastern End in the Year 1823*

Rab Wilson and Calum Colvin, *Burnsiana: Poems and Artworks Inspired by the Life and Legacy of Robert Burns*

Mary Wollstonecraft, *A Vindication of the Rights of Woman*

RECENT TITLES FROM ALICE JAMES BOOKS

The Vault, Andrés Cerpa
White Campion, Donald Revell
Last Days, Tamiko Beyer
If This Is the Age We End Discovery, Rosebud Ben-Oni
Pretty Tripwire, Alessandra Lynch
Inheritance, Taylor Johnson
The Voice of Sheila Chandra, Kazim Ali
Arrow, Sumita Chakraborty
Country, Living, Ira Sadoff
Hot with the Bad Things, Lucia LoTempio
Witch, Philip Matthews
Neck of the Woods, Amy Woolard
Little Envelope of Earth Conditions, Cori A. Winrock
Aviva-No, Shimon Adaf, Translated by Yael Segalovitz
Half/Life: New & Selected Poems, Jeffrey Thomson
Odes to Lithium, Shira Erlichman
Here All Night, Jill McDonough
To the Wren: Collected & New Poems, Jane Mead
Angel Bones, Ilyse Kusnetz
Monsters I Have Been, Kenji C. Liu
Soft Science, Franny Choi
Bicycle in a Ransacked City: An Elegy, Andrés Cerpa
Anaphora, Kevin Goodan
Ghost, like a Place, Iain Haley Pollock
Isako Isako, Mia Ayumi Malhotra
Of Marriage, Nicole Cooley
The English Boat, Donald Revell
We, the Almighty Fires, Anna Rose Welch
DiVida, Monica A. Hand
pray me stay eager, Ellen Doré Watson
Some Say the Lark, Jennifer Chang
Calling a Wolf a Wolf, Kaveh Akbar

Alice James Books is committed to publishing books that matter. The press was founded in 1973 in Boston, Massachusetts as a cooperative, wherein authors performed the day-to-day undertakings of the press. This element remains present today, as authors who publish with the press are invited to collaborate closely in the publication process of their work. AJB remains committed to its founders' original feminist mission, while expanding upon the scope to include all voices and poets who might otherwise go unheard. In keeping with its efforts to build equity and increase inclusivity in publishing and the literary arts, AJB seeks out poets whose writing possesses the range, depth, and ability to cultivate empathy in our world and to dynamically push against silence. The press was named for Alice James, sister to William and Henry, whose extraordinary gift for writing went unrecognized during her lifetime.

Designed by Tiani Kennedy

Printed by McNaughton & Gunn